Moments We Carry

A Collection of Poems on Life's Small Blessings

Alaina McLaughlin

BookLeaf Publishing

India | USA | UK

Made with ❤ on the BookLeaf Publishing Platform
www.bookleafpub.in
www.bookleafpub.com

Dedication

To my family, for filling my life with love and encouragement, and to my mentors, who showed me the beauty of embracing new challenges. Thank you for believing in me and for helping me find the courage to create something new.

Preface

For much of my life, I've defined myself through a single lens—it's been my passion, my purpose, and my identity. But recently, I found myself asking: what happens when we tie ourselves too tightly to one role? Choosing a path that might not lead to the highest ranks has offered both challenges and revelations in my career. Everyone's path to success looks different; the definition of "success" is different for everyone too. These works reflect my journey to explore new passions and the courage to discover different parts of myself with it.

There is nothing earth-shattering in this booklet; there are sources of "everyday magic" everywhere, and I simply started to write about what I was thankful for. I've learned that trying something new is a wonderful way to see what unfolds when we let go of the single thing that we think defines us. This book is a reflection of that mentality: a testament to the power of embracing change, venturing into the unknown, and pursuing what excites you simply because you can. It's been a journey of self-discovery—realizing that identity is not fixed and growth often comes when we allow ourselves the grace to explore.

Acknowledgements

I would like to acknowledge my husband, Daniel, for his endless patience. When I took on this timed poetry writing challenge, I thought it would be easy. He listened to all my poems and reminded me that these don't necessarily have to be a masterpiece. They could be simple, they could be silly, but most importantly, they just had to get done.

Watching the Wetlands Wake Up

Before the dawn, we slipped through foggy air,
A boat adrift in silence, calm and deep,
While shadows held the wetlands in their care,
And murmured tales where ancient waters sleep.

Then came the sun, a ribbon bright and wide,
Its amber light poured softly on the shore.
The cranes, like songs from timeless skies, replied,
Their voices rising as they soared once more.

A hawk loomed briefly by our hiding place,
Then startled eyes met ours in sheer surprise.
While sparrows, bold, approached to see our face,
With fearless hearts, they loitered undisguised.

In silence deep, we watched the day unfold,
As morning's touch revealed a world in gold.

Stepping Into A New World

Far away, the longing burns so bright,

Rising high, it calls me through the night,

Each step ahead gaining more, yet also full of doubt,

Every choice unfolds a world laid out.

Do I dare to wander, bold and free,

Or stay where comfort shields all parts of me?

My heart, divided, seeks the open skies, yet fears the cost

of dreams that dare to rise.

The Comforting Ritual of Togetherness

At dawn, I rise to greet the beasts before
their meowing chorus precedes the sun's light.
We feed them first and then, the peace restored,
my husband acts before the day alights.

He wakes with me, though schedules don't align,
and grinds us fragrant coffee beans to brew.
His taste is keener, refined more than mine;
each blend he picks to start our day anew.

He fills my cup, the steam begins to rise,
and breakfast follows, cooked to my delight.
His tender care—a gift that never dies—
is love wrapped up in each and every bite.

This simple gift, so charming and so sweet,
in every morning, love and life repeat.

A Quiet Refuge

In the noise of their voices,
their accusations, their lies,
I stand silent,
drowning in their judgment.
Each word cuts deeper,
like blades that never miss.

But then I hear you—
the soft hum of love,
unwavering and steady.
You are my shelter,
my quiet refuge from the storm.
You don't see my mistakes as chains
but as lessons in my growth.
Your love, unconditional,
is the balm for my bruised soul.

In a world full of harsh words,
yours are the ones that heal me.

Life's Playlist

A song begins, and my mind starts to race,
A melody full of things I can't erase.
The laughter, the mistakes, the fights I've fought,
All wrapped in a tune, and I'm tangled in thought.

But now I know, as the song softly plays,
There's beauty in lessons, in the messy ways
That people shape us, both good and bad,
In memories we cherish, both happy and sad.

The song is still the same, though much has changed,
And I hear the lessons, the growth, the rearranged.
The words are untouched, but now I hear it differently,
The song's not just history—it's what made me, me.

I've grown from those days, and it's abundantly clear,
The past helped shape the person I am here.
Now I hear the song, and I smile in spite,
For I'm wiser now, and the pangs feel light.

It carries me back to a time long ago,
To moments I lived, to places I'd go.
A journey that's shaped me, made me whole,
A playlist of growth, a song for the soul.

When I hear the song now, it's a melancholy rewind,
But I've learned to let go, to leave that chapter behind.
So when this tune plays, instead I feel more alive,
A reminder of how far I've come, how I've since thrived.

The song comes on and I pause to smile,
Remembering faces I haven't seen in a while.
It's not that I miss them, not in the same way,
But I'm thankful for how they helped me today.

The song is a part of me; when its melody fills the air,
I'm not caught in the past, but just made more aware
That I've blossomed, I've grown, and I'm even more free,
A better version of myself, and all I've come to be.

In the music, the past, the joy of the ride,
I become a better me, with memories as my guide.
And as each song ends, another begins,
New chapters await, with fresh winds and spins.

The future's still writing melodies I have yet to find,
I'll keep adding more songs, expanding my mind.
With every new note, my heart will transcend,
A symphony of life that will never end.

The Softness in Stone

In the quiet of the gallery, I stand,
Before a marble goddess, sculpted by hand.
Her curves aren't smooth, her waist not thin,
Her rounded tummy, a tale of where life's been.
The polished stone glows, imperfect, yet bright,
A tender elegance unveiled in the light.

Her marble skin tells of time's quiet grace,
Of life lived fully, and beauty's embrace.
This statue, this likeness, of a goddess long gone,
Her shape not ideal, but clearly she's strong.
With rounded thighs and a belly that sways,
She defies all the standards the world now would display.

Her stomach is not flat, her hips round and wide,
And in her imperfections, there's beauty inside.
Regarded as a masterpiece and worthy of praise,
She carries her curves in timeless ways.
Her marble body is lauded as a work of art,
Yet its not "perfection" that sets her apart.

Beside me, other women stand in silent thought,
Their gazes tracing the lines the sculptor sought.
In quiet reflection, they look at the stone,
Each one of us pondering the body we own.
We study her softness, her flaws made to shine,
And wonder if we, too, might be considered divine.

The statues stared back, but it was me who wept,
Touched by the beauty that time had kept.
Like the marble, I, too, am a masterpiece,
My flaws don't diminish my beauty or peace.
For in the imperfection, there's magic to find—
A reminder that we are all works of art, and one of a
kind.

Kintsugi of the Soul

A cracked teacup on the shelf, once whole,
Now gleams with gold, its history told.
Where the fracture lay, beauty arose,
In the places broken, something new glows.
I see myself in that repaired line,
Flawed yet perfect, and wholly mine.
Now I look upon my scars with kinder eyes,
As those "flaws" are where my beauty lies.
The gold that fills the cracks I bear,
Is what makes me more than what was once there.

You Are My Atlas to the Weight of Their Words

The weight of their words, heavy as stone,
They blame and accuse as I stand alone.
They whisper of faults, my past on display,
Yet their judgment won't steal my light today.

For in you, my friend, I find my peace,
A love that lets my worries finally cease.
Your heart sees beyond the scars I wear,
You comfort my heart with a presence so rare.

The tongues of others may sting and wound,
But with you beside me, I am soon attuned—
To the truth of your love, pure and clear,
A sound so bright, it vanquishes my fear.

Pages of Escape

Each page a door, each word a key,
Unlocking worlds I long to see.
The world outside may fall away,
But here, I live, if just for today.

Simple Clarity

I step into the room,
And my mood shifts—
The corners, once buried in forgotten piles,
Are clear.
The clutter that once clung to the edges of my thoughts
Is gone.
Now the air feels light,
Like the weight of a thousand small worries has lifted,
Even if only for a moment.

The room is still.
But it brims with promise,
A quiet energy,
One that makes space for deep breaths,
For thoughts to move freely.

I didn't need new furniture,
Nor vibrant colors—
Just a small shift,
A simple order.
Now the mind is free to rest,
And the heart can begin to create again.

Unique Among the Rest

I like a good rock—it doesn't matter where I am, I do enjoy stopping to see what interesting nuggets I can find. Lucky you, you get three poems about rocks: an acrostic, a cinquain, and a haiku. They are simple, but satisfying.

Rocky terrain beneath my feet,
Ornaments of nature, each layer a treat.
Crystal veins and fossilized shells,
Keeping tales alive that time still tells.

Pebble,
shiny and smooth,
quietly resting there.
A magpie stumbles upon it—
treasure.

A unique stone glints,
I pick it up with delight—
Quiet joy unfolds.

Hayan

His fur is almost pure white, but he has a colorful soul;
A yellow and blue gaze that brims with playful energy.
Your company brings him comfort; he offers you peace.
A crooked tail follows him—perfectly imperfect.
Not quite a diamond, but he is priceless to us.

Yeongi

You came into our lives like a whisper, your petite form moving like a shadow.
Elusive at first, but now a constant in our lives—a beloved companion.
Only now do we see the depth of your hard-earned love.
Never demanding, but always deserving—you fill spaces we never knew were empty.
Gentle purrs tell us you've given us your heart, slowly but completely.
In your quiet presence, we find a completeness we never expected.

Writing a booklet is an interesting thing. This is an acrostic, yet the lines spill over. I have edited many of my original poems to fit the confines of this publishing software. Yeongi was a runt—even as an adult, she is a very tiny cat still. However, she has the biggest personality and is absolutely deserving of every single word. Therefore, please enjoy this mashed up acrostic.

The Light Between Us: The Moon's Quiet Promise

The moon hangs above,
a silent witness to all we've ever felt,
its pale light spilling across the world,
bathing everything in its milky light.
I look up at it now, feeling small in the vastness,
yet knowing, in this moment, you too are looking at the
same moon, wherever you are.

On nights when silence feels heavy,
I look up at the moon, its silver face calm in the dark.
I feel connected to something ancient,
something endless.
It doesn't speak, but the moon has seen it all,
witnessing both joy and sorrow,
and in its quiet way, it reminds me that I am part of it all.
Even in the dark, I am not alone.

The moon is a quiet guardian,
casting its light over the world
When everything else around seems dark.
No matter where I am, I can always look up
and find it there,
a silent witness to my thoughts, my hopes, my fears.

I follow the moon's path across the sky,
a silver thread leading me home,
even when home is nowhere in sight.
It lights the way with its silvery cast,
reminding me that no matter where I go,
the moon will always find me.

From wherever I stand,
no matter how far I've wandered,
I know that somewhere, someone else is gazing at the
same sky, finding peace in the same light.
It pulls us together like a thread
that stretches across the skies,
Connected by something larger than time,
no matter how long.
We are simply waiting,
until we meet again beneath its glow.

There's no need for words,
only the simple comfort of knowing,
no matter where we are, we all see this same moon.
It reminds me of all that is constant,
of all that holds us together.
And for this moment, we are not alone.

The Language of Silence

There are no words between us now,
Only silence, and it speaks so loud.
No need for chatter or endless talk,
Just the peace of a silent walk.

Our souls converse without a sound,
No voices in the harmony we found.
It tells of faith, of love, of grace—
A connection so deep, no man can erase.

Seeds of Tomorrow

In the soil of today, I plant the seed,
A dream for tomorrow, a future to feed.
While the dark clouds of yesterday, they still loom,
But sunlight peeks through, dispelling some gloom.
The work may be hard, but the effort will pay,
There's joy in the journey, there's courage in today.
The storms of the past water this garden of hope,
I will learn how to thrive and not just to cope.

Though the past had its trials, its burdens to bear,
The flame of tomorrow is burning somewhere.
Each step is a promise, a path to explore,
And what is to come is worth waiting for.
I nurture the seeds by giving myself grace,
For I know they'll soon grow in this brighter space.
For now, tomorrow's horizon is waiting for me,
And I cannot wait to become all I was meant to be.

Elements of Love

He pours my coffee as the daylight creeps,
While I sleep on, his care my morning sun.
The warmth he gives, a promise that he keeps,
A love that wakes me before the day's begun.

As rain falls soft upon the parched ground,
His presence nourishes and revives my soul.
Through droughts and storms, he's always around,
His love flows freely and makes me whole.

He is the wind beneath my soaring wings,
A gentle breeze that uplifts and carries me along.
Together, we adapt to what life brings,
Through all we face, our love stays strong.

The world may tremble, but he will not sway,
He is the foundation where faith and love are sown.
Through thick or thin, I get a kiss to end the day
A rock on which our family's love has grown.

Joyful Melody

There once was a thrush in a tree,
Whose song was as sweet as can be.
It sang all day long,
A beautiful song,
And it filled all the world with such glee.

The Jolly Robin's Jig

A robin bops on the dewy morning grass,
Fluffing its feathers with a merry bit of sass.
With a hop and a jump,
It wiggles its rump,
Singing sweet songs as others flit past.

Where Peace Begins

A part of me I once held tight,
I set it free into the night.
And though it seemed like letting go,
I found that peace began to grow.
Perfection's chains began to break,
And in their stead, joy took its place.
No longer chasing, no more strife,
The magic was in a simpler life.

A Memory Etched in the Sky

A star burned brightly in one swift streak,
So dazzling, so bold, and so unique.
In a flash, the comet was gone,
But a reminder of it still lingers on.
Though it has since faded out of view,
Its light within me still shines through.
That fleeting star I'll always find,
A memory bright, etched in my mind.